WE VAGABONDS

WE VAGABONDS

Poems by Diane Marquart Moore

Copyright © 2020 Diane Marquart Moore

Border Press
PO Box 3124
Sewanee, Tennessee 37375
www.borderpressbooks.com
victoria@borderpressbooks.com

All rights reserved. No part of this book may be used in any manner without written permission.

ISBN: 978-1-7346802-1-8
Library of Congress Control Number: 2020938915

Cover image from watercolor on paper by Jean Claire Barlow Wattigny, 1984

Printed in the United States

To Victoria I. Sullivan

"As soon as I saw you I knew a grand adventure was about to happen."

— Winnie the Pooh —

CONTENT

We Vagabonds
Travel with Grandma
Staying in One Place
As Well at Home
High Country, North Carolina
Patio Leaves
The Vagabond Armadillo
West Wings
Part II.
When The Coronavirus Came
II
III
IV
V
The Circus Master
Runaway
Still Cloistered
What the Chinese Willed To Us
Part III.
The Border States
What Are They Looking For?
Beginning Of "Vagabondage"
Looking Back
Possum Kingdom, Texas
Ocean Springs, Mississippi
Land of the Little People
Georgia
Big Sur
Afternoon in Sedona, Arizona
The Red Hills of Home, Brandon, Mississippi
Aroostook County, Maine
The Road to Cowan, Tennessee

801 Draper Rd., Blacksburg, Virginia
Shakers Who Gave Their Hearts To God
Eureka Springs, Arkansas
Biography

ALSO BY DIANE MARQUART MOORE

POETRY
- An Ordinary Day
- Field Marks
- Consolation of Gardens
- Ultimate Pursuit
- All Love,
- Let the Trees Answer
- Spring's Kiss
- Above the Prairie
- Sifting Red Dirt
- A Slow Moving Stream
- Street Sketches
- Corner of Birch Street
- Strand of Beads
- A Lonely Grandmother
- Between Plants and Humans
- Night Offices
- Departures
- In a Convent Garden
- Mystical Forest
- Everything is Blue
- Post Cards From Diddy Wah Diddy
- Alchemy
- Old Ridges
- Rising Water
- The Holy Present and Farda
- Grandma's Good War
- Afternoons in Oaxaca (Las Poesias)
- The Book of Uncommon Poetry
- Counterpoint
- Your Chin Doesn't Want to Marry
- Soaring

More Crows
Just Passing Through
Moment Seized

YOUNG ADULTS
Martin and the Last Tribe
Martin Finds His Totem
Flood on the Rio Teche
Sophie's Sojourn in Persia
Kajun Kween
Martin's Quest

ADULT FICTION
Redeemed by Blood
Silence Never Betrays
Chant of Death with Isabel Anders
Goat Man Murder
The Maine Event
Nothing for Free

CHILDREN
The Beast Beelzebufo
The Cajun Express

NON-FICTION
Porch Posts with Janet Faulk-Gonzales
Iran: In A Persian Market
Their Adventurous Will
Live Oak Gardens
Treasures of Avery Island

WE VAGABONDS

Will wind end it all
instead of fire or ice?

Ask the trees in Enterprise, Alabama,
great roots exposed, gasping for life

beside the wild flowing Chunky River;
They show disdain wind has for pines,

toppling the tallest,
death with an acrid scent,

fallen needles for miles
my father's declaration carried on its breath:

We will be gypsies,
home is forever moving.

And we are blown into rain,
queens of the road,

vagabonds with three homes
to keep and run away from

because the wind destroys
what we strain to keep,

our vain attempts at voyage…
to bring distance home.

TRAVEL WITH GRANDMA

He traveled under new suns
counted forty states, Canada and Mexico,

but in the van drew an exact replica
of one of his heavy shoes.

A wish on a piece of copy paper:
please stop the van

so I can step into these shoes,
walk the rest of the way home.

STAYING IN ONE PLACE

Expectations come from staying
in one place, a comfortless monotony

cleaning, cooking, wearing a robe all day
the litany of requests for social visits,

formalities of communal life.
How many domesticities hinder vigor

until we revolt by poem,
ponder if what we birthed

was good for this world,
catharsis and transformation

by chance happening without ardor,
wool gathering while staying in place.

AS WELL AT HOME

What I see of butterweed and fleabane
following the compass of the spirit

does not enliven me
any more than basil and thyme

now brown and tired
in their bed at Sewanee;

St. Francis has been overturned,
wind having upended him

and sent a cedar limb akimbo
into the roof of my home.

For a week, my world faltered,
then resumed, a vision

of humus in a bag
coming to me,

the serious hum of locusts
returning to my ears.

There was no end to these things,
they had not been done in, done for.

I saw tenacious ladybugs
clustering in corners

of warm rooms indoors
and were they fornicating

or foretelling a cold spring,
cautious and melancholy?

No matter. We will break ground
after the purple thistle

and white haired clover
effortlessly pass on

unworried about posterity,
sacred journey complete.

HIGH COUNTRY, NORTH CAROLINA

I.

Everything is connected. An old Irish proverb says "mountains never meet but people can always encounter each other." At midnight I'm praying about my daughter's anxiety and insomnia, whose anxiety and insomnia become my own. At dawn, I awaken in a motel room and go to the window. The green firs shiver on the mountaintop. They have been awake all night. The room is empty and silent. At midmorning I enter a dulcimer shop, and a smiling woman with reddish blond hair gives me a lesson on a homemade dulcimer made with a tomato can. She is from Crystal Springs, Mississippi, burial ground of my former husband's grandmother. I tell her about my daughter's insomnia and she reveals she has suffered from it, that she takes medication for her anxiety. Her fine smile disappears. I leave the shop without a walnut dulcimer I wish I could purchase one so I can pretend that I am like Rumi and recite poems against the sounds of a stringed instrument in the dark…for my daughter and for all who don't sleep because fear travels in the darkness. After lunch, I go into the chapel of St. Mary of the Hills and pray, lighting a candle at a *prie dieu* in a corner that commemorates the Holocaust, a time when there was never a night of peaceful sleep. I watch the candle flicker and feel that the problem is solved. At 4:30 p.m. the telephone rings. It is my daughter who sounds relieved and calm. "The doctor prescribed medication" she said. "I won't resist the medicine. When I told the doctor I hadn't slept for a year she said that the loss of sleep for such a long time would make anyone off-center." The medication was the same as the one that the woman in the dulcimer shop had revealed she was taking. I went to the window and looked at the firs on the mountain top. They were no longer shivering, and the wind had died. I felt calm and thought about how everything is connected by a universe of hands, connected by a universe of prayers, connected by The One who never sleeps…and is never restless.

II.

At Blowing Rock, I read the story about two native American lovers, a Chickasaw maiden and a Cherokee brave who wandered into the maiden's province. When the brave decided to return to his people, he departed from a high rock and traveled through a flume powered by the northwest wind, and the wind swept him back upward into the arms of the beloved. Was it an ancient wind that no longer knew which way to blow?

PATIO LEAVES

I can sweep away leaves
but not the *memento mori;*

are they blown in or drift down
from the umbrella above —

a dangerous shelter
or many seasons' grace?

The scatter of brittle brown
clutters the patio all year

fallen from a venerable oak,
a parent who bestows perpetual treasure;

leaves beckoning me to sweep,
the oak's fingers inviting

scuttling squirrels who
make their own tempest,

shake limbs free of leaf…
bad tenants without brooms.

THE VAGABOND ARMADILLO

Another lumbering descendant
of glyptodonts sighted in the backyard,

a brazen carrier of leprosy
trafficked over from Texas,

at my appearance jumps
high into the humid air

and scurries into his home
in the coulee.

I wish I could transport him
to Oaxaca City,

my favorite Mexican haunt,
where he's served up as a prized dish,

but also famed as the Hoover hog

rustled up by an ancient Model T

hurtling through dense woods,
hunted down by my father-in-law

and consumed during the Great Depression.
Never grunting, squealing,

silently scooping up termites
as if consuming human sins

enclosed in the house beside him;
never assured of angel wings

wearing his heavy plated armor.
He could be first cousin

to the pangolin lately accused
of spreading the killer epidemic,

Coronavirus,
could be trapped in the company

of beasts, diabolic critters,
could even be a species of pink fairies

sent to warn us
of a backyard Armageddon?

WEST WINGS

Should I go on singing Happy Trails,
contradictory music for my feelings
when, at 17, you boarded a bus
bound for sunny L.A. with a black man?
Or should I rage at your deranged
adolescence, an early immigration
crossing borders without permission?
I put on black in heavy weather,
the *forever-after* nest empty
of unruly child, another vagabond
born into a wayward family.
I hold my breath
as you still dwell within me,
my fierce mother heart grieving
as deeply as the day you ran away
on those short legs to join
what you perceived as
the wagon train of your dreams.

PART II.

WHEN THE CORONAVIRUS CAME

We returned from the road
and found trees fallen, a sudden sweep
having uprooted a giant pine,
sap dripping from its sides,
roots splayed like dead fingers.

A vision of Job stepped out,
took his place beside the roots,
this blameless man,
wild-haired and muddy,
now repeating:

"The Lord gave, the Lord took,"
but first, "the Lord gave,"
not speaking of those calamities
that had beset him,
had not matched his character.

He stood there withdrawn,

waiting for God to speak again
his survival diminished
by a large fallen tree,
a vision not convincing enough

for me to bear what he had borne,
not enough for me to trust
the exhalation of God's breath —
a whirlwind tossing trees,
cheeks filled with disease and death.

II.

We are allowed to walk alone outdoors,
travel suspended like waning violets
fields blooming between March and May
but the Unconscious keeps going,
horror becomes the memory of "the old days."
We lack rational life,

keep everything past arm's length,
every day a danger,
sleep while erect
look through an album
of colored travel photos
hoping something will move

from within an experience,
our wandering spirits
knowing we have no time to lose
except in the night
when we settle old accounts.

III.

Time gone forever
not lost in antiquity,
Greek marble busts,
ashes of former gods
and dead civilizations,
but only a few months ago;
this distance of six feet
between each of us,
a step back for true perspective?

IV.

Our present president thinks
he can repair the universe
envisions himself as Atlas
holding up the sky
but is really the emperor
without any clothes
walking in puddles
with his arms above his neck.

V.

Questions…

Did I dream we traveled monthly
spent years on all those roads?
I hold onto scenes
passing through my mind
roads still there
while I feel far away
from places I've left
but remain in safekeeping
between my prayers.
Like falling stars
the spirit moves ahead
taking chances,
an eye witness within…
But we desperate turtles
pace in the yard,
heads withdrawn
miles between each other
(remember we can walk alone),
and will we become museum pieces

when the weather changes?
How does it feel when we're
unable to catch our breath?
What will soothe and shape our lives
after global despair?
Will language die?
Can time be saved
or erased?
Creation have a second round?

THE CIRCUS MASTER

In our country old before its time
we walk more slowly each day,
a neighborhood of loners;
no leaning out of windows
and haloing across the divide,
created by a fall in the garden again
misled, misguided
by an aspiring demagogue waving
from a purple and gold float,
orange hair edging his clown face,
gloved hands throwing trinkets
to us — bareback riders
suddenly become captive
in homes without season
willing to plunge into any fire ring
to escape the succession of his lies.

RUNAWAY

He wasn't the first family runaway;
Brother Paul, at three, found "pishing,"
cane pole in hand on a creek bank,
I, at 12, pedaled my bicycle to a city bus stop
got as far as a Greyhound bus station;
daughter Elizabeth, at 17, bound
for California on another Greyhound
and, I might add, domiciled there 37 years.
(Sometimes they never come back).
Now, Alexander Charles, age nine,
weary of indoor pursuits with twin sisters,
imprisoned during the Coronavirus plague,
crept out of his bed and sped away
piloting a battery-operated motor scooter.
Lively with imagination, smartest of all of us,
caught by his mother cruising
the posh neighborhood in her Honda,
braked his vehicle and explained the flight:
"They say Vitamin D is really good
for keeping away the virus."
Smart, lively with imagination,

Alexander Charles, banished to his room…
Again.
Today, I received a video of his sister Kate,
four-year old legs pedaling fast
on a new bicycle with training wheels,
saying to her parents "I can do it myself,.."

Next.

STILL CLOISTERED

Quarantined. Silence reigns.
The house smells of dust —
the stuff of abandonment.
No one rings the doorbell,
if they do, our feet back away,
this is the new way to love.
Space banks itself in all the rooms,
the old maps destroyed.
Losses are random
but don't look back, they say,
keep your mind shuttered,
we can't escape hope
we've kept our resolutions of isolation.
The old/new leitmotif reigns: life shifts
and the Mardi Gras parades end
but don't be ungracious about a purge,
the heart remains exposed,
its appeal still alive in the empty streets.

WHAT THE CHINESE WILLED TO US

(THE CORONAVIRUS)

We no longer exist,
opinions lost,
friends, relatives washed away
in colonies of age and pain
by a name foreign to well-being,
imprisoned in history
no one cares to record
while we sit on the sofa
protesting, defending,
put in place
trying to bring distance home,
wondering if we've ever been.

PART III.

THE BORDER STATES

In each place we visited I left no imprint
but it became my roots:
Georgia, Alabama, North and South Carolina,
states that touched middle Tennessee,
the world I called my own.

Now when white daffodils have finished
I am imprisoned,
look out from a smeared window,
a view I took for granted,
trees now dropping white and pink blossoms,

the air thick with pollen,
islands of light
shining with the green of spring —
magic out there
among all the broken promises.

I dream of the road
after a sleepless night
living without choices, unregenerate,

the room heavy with biblical prophecy,
stealthy prey hiding on my doorstep.

WHAT ARE THEY LOOKING FOR?

Crows looking like aged ministers
fly into a murky sky
foretelling drear ahead,
mocking my silent prayers;

a murder of atheists they hover,
one flap away from being carrion
eying my silver earrings
on a table beside my bed.

Once, they followed me to Mexico,
landing in Monterey's Chipinque,
the arms of dense pines
in a park of butterflies and woodpeckers.

Lost souls without destination
they skirted an abandoned zoo
like us, seeking tradition, connection…
travelers out of work.

BEGINNING OF "VAGABONDAGE"

(Desert enroute to California, Age 11)

This long expanse of land
made me feel less enclosed
after weeks in a Ford coupe and Army tent;
cottonwoods shimmering in a slight wind
that blew through its wide leaves

and in the long stretches of mesa
coyotes lurked along arroyos,
lonesome looking mountains
looming over them in the distance.
We rode and rode,

never seemed to near the peaks

but anticipated reaching them,
saw them come out of their hiding place.
At night a jackrabbit leapt into view,
our headlights illuminating greasewood roots;

He escaped my father for a moment,
long ears poised like tv antennas
until the crack of a rifle brought him down
barbecued jackrabbit for breakfast, father said,
daylight revealing rabbit and tumbleweed
carcasses warming our hood.

LOOKING BACK

My mother waited for something to appear
over the next hill, the coupe
spinning like a shiny blue top,
Texas landscape unwinding
toward beckoning Lake Buchanan,

rocky limestone hills,
oak, juniper, mesquite Savannahs,
native rock houses spaced far apart,
goats, hooves poised on mesquite trunks
and grazing on their leaflets;

There, one of the most ancient
geological regions in the world,
outcroppings of granite
guarding small water oaks,
the ubiquitous prickly pear

scarring landscape to which I've returned
again and again over eighty years,
the car racing toward a life of uncertainty

a future of water bags on the hood
gray utility trailer slapping the road behind.

We thought we had entered Paradise
at Twenty Nine Palms,
followed mirages, seas of yellow sand
a lilac haze overhanging,
sometimes turning pink

the color of my parents' dreams,
but we applauded when my father
turned the steering wheel in Beverly Hills
and we emerged from a roller coaster,
weary vagabonds

always looking back like Harold Jr.
who coined the word "oohgone"
as we sped past windmills spinning
above the vast desert landscapes,
family life disappearing on the wind.

POSSUM KINGDOM, TEXAS

She runs from me through dry grass,
tangled blond hair flying,
my daughter at three,
afraid of shampoo since infancy
begs me not to wash her hair,

emerald eyes only calm when asleep
as before she was born,
holds out her arms to someone
to whom she has given her whole heart
and betrayed by a bottle of soap;

I tell her about possums
living on a lake a few miles away
that sound like her, crybaby,
good creatures that eat rats and snakes
and never have to wash their hair;

She looks up, wary,

tries to heal herself,
the voice of fear
always attempting to claim her
suddenly soothed with lore

about a kingdom of creatures
that safeguard her,
now washes her hair without pain,
believes in something she never left behind
and has no idea what it is.

OCEAN SPRINGS, MISSISSIPPI

For two years we went there each month,
sea gulls, sea air, seasons of thunder surrounding,
saw Walter Anderson walking the shore
of the Gulf, dreaming of being in his boat
rowing out to Horn Island

the beginning and ending of his world
before the wind died down;
pelicans, turtles, blue crabs
settling on his brush tip
in the place to which he returned

to sweep his memory clean,
a storm blowing up in his mind
where he felt passion,
escaped into the unknown again,
journeying through a curtain of sand

to freedom and while there

welcoming the result of his madness,
this landscape he could paint
like the sky bursting with red clouds
emptying him of the terrible emptiness.

LAND OF THE LITTLE PEOPLE

Sylva, North Carolina,
name like light glinting on metal,
home of Cherokee legends,
masks of frogs coming out of a man's mouth,
stories about possums losing their tails;

the Cherokees who believed
that balance was the path of true being,
life for the good of the whole,
were fascinated by their own tales
about the Little People, Moon People

with red whiskers and blue skin
the faces of elves with big ears
who came out only at night,
lived underground, traveled in four feet tunnels,
emerging by moonlight to do their gardening.

Protectors or mischief makers? no one really knew,

beings never having been born, never dying,
spirits usually unseen, said to be
maybe little men hiding under porches
making strange noises.

They put spells on food
bad deeds returning to haunt
those who lived out of balance,
People mysteriously died
who dared to mention their existence.

GEORGIA

For me, the state was all agriculture,
an engagement with the land,
stewards of farm fresh food
from Blue Ridge to Lower Coastal Plain:
apples, peaches, pumpkins and sweet corn,
free range, grass fed, U-Picks;

but we missed the Plains Peanut Festival
President Jimmy Carter signing books
and holding forth about peanuts.
My Virginia farm ancestry reared its head
each time I smelled Fuji, Delicious, and Cameo,
apples fruity and melony,

fried pies, cobbler and apple butter
celebrating all that was fresh
from the soil for the soul,
fresh ground grits for breakfast
with a hollow of home made butter,
rock music blaring in the orchard

to frighten off wild hogs and deer,
no artificial flavor or color,
the icon of sustainability
and a label that read *Georgia Certified*
like an inspection sticker
plastered on our windshield.

BIG SUR

Rock lagoons in the Pacific Valley
remind me my life is a guano boulder,
an accretion of tragedy I move through
to reach the redolent eucalyptus grove,
Gorda Springs by the sea;

distant mountains burn to yellow straw
relentless sun baking them
and cacti below, stalactites spiking upward
as my hapless psyche
straining to color the universe.

Look at the driftwood, my brother said,
yes, I answered, *come up from ocean depths,*
like us, refugees from the harsh tide,
and with age, our roads have no destinations,
realize they are going nowhere.

AFTERNOON IN SEDONA, ARIZONA

The desert is a lonely place
but there you can take you
into your own world
look up at a wall of red rock
meditate on what is real,
what is imagined,
a continent of being
absorbing all time, no time,
this long conversation between wall
and mind, constant red slate rising
like sunset cacti laced with spines,
broken pieces of Self,
a momentary universe.

THE RED HILLS OF HOME, BRANDON, MISSISSIPPI

We thought we were on our way
racing to join Dora Runnels in heaven?
A well-meaning church woman
who drove us to Brandon cemetery
turned into the path of an oncoming car
and swerved just in time;
jays screaming as we made the turn,
death pounding toward us,
red clay hills ready to lay claim
to what was not meant to be.
Tall pines whispered Dora's religious verse,
a monotone of superstition
going in the opposite direction
from my belief in *mysterium tremendum,*
*and t*he instant we turned I envisioned
ivy climbing the walls of an orderly place,
rocks worn smooth in the yard,
and inside Dora's house
the kitchen table emanating smells

of supper the preceding night,
rooms holding her disdain for a religion
without wormwood and gall,
this puritan stranger, great-grandmother
mocking what she called
my *Anglican liturgical extravagance* —
sacrilege in the red hills of home.

AROOSTOOK COUNTY, MAINE

No smell of funeral flowers
those ground frozen days
too deep for natives to bury their dead,
bodies stacked in mausoleums,
coffin makers out of work,
gravesites vacant;

Surreal to be there
looking for a sun that never shone,
snow piled against telephone poles
no soil in sight,
indoors the sound of a scratched recording
of Tchaikovsky's 5th playing;

an oil stove flickered
while we walked room to room
heavy steps climbed the outer stairs
seeking company for coffee, cigarettes,
a lively game of Canasta.

I longed to hear crickets' monotonous sawing,

to raise a window and let in
the scent of lilacs, a gentle wind soughing
in the great alluvial valley of the Mississippi.
In May, when the snow melted
we looked for a spot of grass on the hill
and found a cracked flower pot beside the door.

THE ROAD TO COWAN, TENNESSEE

When spring stirs, we travel;
all else failing, to Cowan Tennessee,
hawks drifting overhead,

wings shuddering now and then,
the road spiraling downward
reminding me of the highway to Big Sur;

and where the ocean would be
sycamore, maple rise, thick fog hovers
like heavy mist overlooking the Pacific.

Near Cowan, a large pond
becomes landing point of Canadian Geese,
entry to a town relaxed, forgotten,

a field of planted corn now flooded,
water running muddy, the crop
no longer growing into sweetness.

There is no morality in nature's proclivities,
fencing in the rain
and unsettling a fragile field;

We reach this town where steam locomotives
traveled a 2200 foot tunnel
Irishmen blasted through tons of rock,

clouds of black smoke
following a locomotive
that plunged down a steep grade;

A feeling of eeriness
pursues our approach
like a pusher gathering steam

as we descend to the known,
Cowan, when all else fails…
and we wonder why the train doesn't come.

801 DRAPER RD., BLACKSBURG, VIRGINIA

A mound of linen, silver, and candelabra,
I inherited photographs of table service and cats
than the humans who lived there

among delusions of grandeur,
one photograph of me visiting, clad in fur,
their version of an adopted daughter;

upstairs, Josephine, their black cook
photographed taking orders for dinner
from the queen lying in a tester bed:

baked chicken and dressing, "Bam's rolls",
cucumber aspic and fresh peach cobbler,
Oysters Rockefeller on a sideboard of crystal.

Outside they planted a weeping willow
I had claimed as my favorite tree,
a rose garden and lattice of wisteria;

The mirror in the dining room
reflected no faces,
only a crystal chandelier from France;

It hung alongside the portrait of a woman
wearing a plunging neckline of russet velvet,
breasts — godmother's idea of sophisticated metier.

They willed this brazen likeness to her alma mater,
a women's university touted as grand place
of her delusions, now a hotbed of feminists…

"primitives," she would have denounced them,
common women without culture or class
in need of her kind of glamour.

All these accouterments of elegance and bondage
my godparents promised to leave behind for me
their purebred kin…and fortunately did not.

SHAKERS WHO GAVE THEIR HEARTS TO GOD

PLEASANT HILL, KENTUCKY

They shook themselves free
of sin and sloth, social evils,
embraced industry, honesty, simplicity,
performing their work as if they had
one thousand years to live,

as if they'd die tomorrow,
believers in the New Lebanon
they built from quarried rock.
They were cautioned not to carry two faces,
to clean their rooms so well

spirits could move in and live there.
The Sisters warped their own silk
saving even the cocoon for kerchiefs

worn during their sacred dance
stomping, traversing up and down,

shaking the floors of a meeting room,
Black and White making joyful noises,
shrieking and yelling their spiritual gifts
and returning to work of highest use…
best known as God's greatest beauty.

EUREKA SPRINGS, ARKANSAS

I took her away from bad influences,
Eureka, I thought, name for miracle expected;
Eureka, new beginning for Adolescent Resistance
where Christ of the Ozarks held out his arms
above a Penthouse Suite in a Gothic hotel,
stood, unsmiling, in the land of healing waters.
while she looked down on gingerbread houses,
discovered the home of Carrie Nation,
face of prohibition, icon of rebellious spirit.

My daughter, her head drooping on my shoulder,
as live horses entered the scene of the Passion Play,
dropped excrement below,
warning us of this Eureka moment.
Something precious about to be lost.
Eureka I thought, she has been converted,
Eureka she thought,
that is my exit word for running away.
and nothing lasts that is forced.

AUTHOR

Diane Marquart Moore is a poet, journalist, an author of fiction and nonfiction, and a blogger at "A Word's Worth." She regularly contributes to the *Pinyon Review*, has published in *The Southwestern Review Interdisciplinary Humanities* (University of Louisiana, Lafayette, Louisiana), *The Xavier Review, Acadiana Profile Magazine, American Weave, Louisiana Historical Review, Trace,* among others. During the reign of the Shahanshah in Iran, she reviewed books and wrote articles for The *Yaddasht Haftegy* (The National Iranian Oil Company journal) in Ahwaz. She retired as archdeacon of the Episcopal Diocese of Western Louisiana and divides her time between Sewanee, Tennessee and New Iberia, Louisiana.

We hope you enjoyed reading this Border Press book

If you would like to read more books and ebooks of poetry by Diane Marquart Moore, please email victoria@borderpressbooks.com to subscribe to our mailing list. Also, please go to www.borderpressbooks.com to learn about books in other genre published by Border Press Books.